EARLY AEROPLANES

THIS IS THE FIRST volume in a series designed to cover the history of the aeroplane from the earliest days to the present.

Flying machines fascinated men for many centuries before anyone managed to fly. Despite the plans of Da Vinci, who intended to reproduce by mechanical means the flapping of a bird's wings, and the early planes powered by steam engines, it was not until the invention of the internal combustion engine that anyone became airborne, in other than balloons, airships or gliders.

Any history of the early days of flying must of necessity be dominated by the Wright brothers. The exciting events at Kill Devil Hills are fully described. But many machines were being developed in Europe at the same time, and both France and England were in the forefront during these pioneering years. Of the many 'firsts' described in this book are Blèriot's Channel Flight and the first launching of a plane from a moving ship—H.M.S. *Hibernia*.

Also in this Series

AEROPLANES OF WORLD WAR I

AEROPLANES 1919–1939

By HOWARD LINECAR AND DONALD GREEN

[*opposite*]
The Avro 504 two-seater biplane of 1913–1914

HOWARD LINECAR

EARLY AEROPLANES

Illustrated by DONALD GREEN

LONDON · ERNEST BENN LIMITED

First published 1965 by Ernest Benn Limited
Bouverie House, Fleet Street, London, EC4

Second impression 1970

© *Howard W. A. Linecar & Donald Green 1965*

Printed in Great Britain

510–13101–8

Contents

List of Illustrations

Acknowledgement

I SHOULD LIKE to thank Charles Gibbs-Smith for his book, *The Aeroplane: an historical survey*, from which most of the facts in this story were obtained. My thanks are also due to the Librarian of the American Embassy, London, to the Smithsonian Institution, Washington, to Commander Tuck of the Science Museum, London, and to P. R. Jempson of Bristol Siddeley Engines, Ltd., Filton, for extensive notes on the rotary engine. Responsibility for the final text attaches to the author, and to him alone.

1965.   H.L.

CHAPTER I

The First Attempts

FROM the earliest times, man has always wanted to fly. The sight of birds, soaring and gliding effortlessly through the air has always been a challenge. In the dim ages of legend stories were told of efforts to fly. From the Ancient Greeks and from the still older Egyptian civilisation have come tales of man's attempts to take to the air. Angels and Sacred Beings are commonly endowed with that mysterious power which men have for so long envied, the power of flight.

In order to make human flight possible there were many who experimented. Among them was the painter and early scientist, Leonardo da Vinci (1452–1516). Five hundred years ago he designed and built model flying machines. Throughout the history of flying half of the problem has been to discover a light and compact supply of power that would make the machine fly. It was not till the petrol engine was developed that such a power became available.

In the carpenter's shop at school most of us have used a bow saw, and noted the twisted cord with a piece of wood through it that held the blade under tension. Most of us have twisted a similar piece of string with wood through it, or with a weight at one end, and watched the way the wood or weight revolved when released. Many of us have played with a toy consisting of a twisted metal rod with a propeller threaded on it. When the propeller was pushed quickly upwards till it shot off the top of the twisted rod, it sailed through the air till the power that started it was exhausted. Not a few of us have taken a watch or clock to pieces, and had the spring fly open before we could prevent it. Here are three simple sources of power: twisted string, twisted metal rod, and twisted metal strip: all storing up power. Da Vinci knew these, and tried to use them to make his models fly. Some of his machines had wings that flapped. Some had blades which revolved like the airscrew of a helicopter. It is just possible that one of his model helicopters did make a short flight. It was only a screw-shaped propeller, but it may have flown. Proof of the fact is lacking.

Over the centuries many experimenters built wing-shaped machines which they hoped would

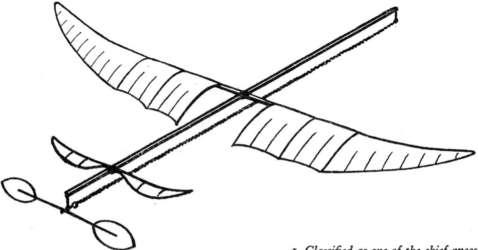

1. Classified as one of the chief ancestors of the modern aeroplane, Pénaud's model of 1871. The airscrew at the back was driven by twisted rubber, now dignified by the title of 'rubber motor'

fly. Though they were in different shapes and sizes, many of them were related to the paper dart which we still throw into the air in the classroom when the teacher's back is turned. Without any machine to drive these shapes along and keep them flying, man naturally tried the strength of his own arms and legs as a possible supply of power. Even today this supply of power is still being tried, though no flying machine so far built has remained in the air for long when powered by arms and legs.

The only other way of flying that looked possible was to glide. Here again, many people built wing-shaped machines, got into them and jumped from high buildings or ran down steep hills till they became airborne. Such flights did not last for long. It was not till modern times that man realised that to keep a glider in the air for any length of time needed more than just a wing-shaped machine. It also needed the knowledge of the use of up-currents of air, rising from the ground. Such currents of warm air, known as thermals, heated by contact with the earth and rising like invisible fountains, were unknown to the early experimenters with flying.

But the men who fitted themselves with 'wings' and ran down steep hills till their feet left the ground had the right idea, and were the first of the flyers. One of these was Sir George Cayley (1773–1857), a Yorkshireman who is now regarded as the 'father of flying'. He had many right ideas about flight. About 1852 he built a machine of the type which we should now call a glider. With this he managed to get a man flying, and was the first to do so. He persuaded a boy who worked for him to be his pilot. Pleased at the success of getting the boy off the ground, he next tackled his coachman. You can well imagine that this man, used to the security of the firm driving seat of a coach, with horses in front and good, strong wheels under him,

was not at all pleased when his master asked him to fly. But he tried it, and was thus, so far as we know, the first man to fly. But the experience must have frightened him, and he left Sir George's employment soon afterwards.

Sir George was full of bright ideas. He realised the lack of some source of mechanical power. He tried his hand at making an engine driven by gunpowder. This did not work very well, probably because of the amount of ash which was produced, and which was not easy to get rid of. Unlike the exhaust produced from a petrol or diesel engine it was solid, and would not just drift away into the air. He also had ideas about a jet engine, but this was never built, and neither of these engines was used in his attempts to fly.

In the meantime, Newcomen, Murdoch, Watt, Stephenson, and many others were experimenting with and improving the steam engine. They put it

2. Cayley's model glider of 1804. This glider is now generally accepted as the first modern aeroplane

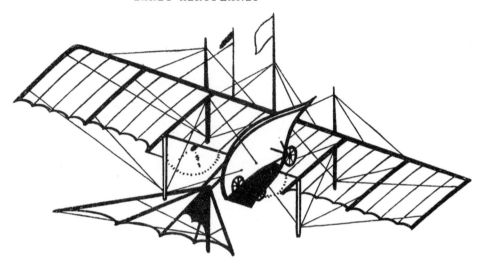

3. Henson's Aerial Steam Carriage, patented in 1842–3

on wheels and made it run on the roads and on rails. More than this, they made it pull many times its own weight. Seeing this, the experimenters with flying thought they had found a source of power that would keep their flying machines in the air. Many of them tried it, but it was too heavy to keep itself up in the air. One or two steam powered machines did get off the ground, but none of them *really* flew. This was a disap-pointment, as the builders of balloons and air-ships were having some success with steam powered machines. The difference was that they carried their steam engines aloft hung below a bag full of lighter-than-air gas, and then drove the bag forward by steam engine and propeller. But the steam engine would not lift its own weight, and the weight of a set of wings, plus the weight of one or more men.

Apart from steam, most other known sources of power were tried in attempts to fly. Compressed air, clockwork, gunpowder, blank cartridges, twisted string and rubber, carbonic acid gas, pedalling like a bicycle: anything that looked like a source of power was tried out, but with no real success.

While all this was going on, Lenoir, Diesel, Daimler and others were inventing and developing the gas and oil engine in various forms, and laying the foundations of the petrol and diesel engines of today. Their engines were tried in flying machines, and some chances of success at last began to come into sight.

Two main principles now had to be brought together. The work of those who experimented

4. The father of modern flying. Otto Lilienthal flying one of his monoplane gliders in 1895

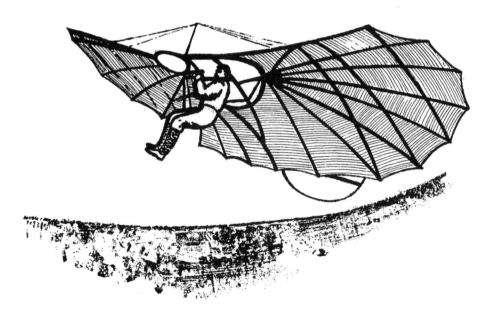

with gliding: Cayley, Lilienthal, Pilcher, Chanute and many others, had to be joined to the work of the experimenters with petrol engines. S. P. Langley and the brothers, Wilbur and Orville Wright studied to bring these two separate experiments together, and we shall now see how this was done.

To follow the story through we should take a quick look at some of the machines which the early experimenters designed or built. Many of them were quite remarkable. A lot of them were only models. Others were intended to be man-carrying. Most of them contributed something to the total of flying knowledge, if only a proof that their design was faulty.

Among the steam enthusiasts was F. D. Artingstall who, in 1830, built a wing-flapping machine. When he tried to make it fly it flapped itself to pieces and finally exploded. Twelve years later another steam power addict built a helicopter whose blades were made to revolve by jets of steam blown out of the blade tips. He seems to have been in advance of his time with his model, but to have had right ideas. The model did manage briefly to get off the ground.

A partnership between W. S. Henson and John Stringfellow produced a 20-ft. span model aeroplane, which was tested at Chard in Somerset in 1847. Again the steam engine was too heavy, and in spite of its two pusher-propellers the model only power-glided to the ground. Henson followed this machine with a smaller, 10-ft. span, steam driven model in 1848. There is no proof that this ever flew.

A French naval officer, Du Temple, built a clockwork driven model, later changing its power supply to steam. This not only flew for a few moments but landed safely, and therefore is considered as the 'first powered aeroplane to sustain itself in the air'. He also built the first powered, full-size aeroplane ever constructed, in 1857. It is not now known if this was driven by hot air or steam, but after a 'running start' it *just* got off the ground and was the first powered, man-carrying aircraft to do so. It was not really a success.

In Glasgow, J. M. Kaufmann built another steam driven 'flapper' which, like that of Artingstall, broke up on test. Another, working in the same way, was built by Forlanini in 1877, and this did manage to get into the air. A model aeroplane powered by compressed air was built in 1879, and managed a short flight.

A Frenchman, Clement Ader, built a steam-driven, bat-like machine, which he tested in 1890, but it never quite flew. He followed it with another, the Avion III. This also never flew, though observers of its tests said that part of its weight was borne by the wings, but it never really got into the air.

Sir Hiram S. Maxim, a naturalised American,

5. Sir Hiram Maxim's steam driven aeroplane of 1894. This expensive test-rig was not intended to fly, but to investigate the problems of power, thrust, and lift. The investigation cost almost £20,000. After the third test run experiments were abandoned

now came on the scene. At great expense he produced in 1894 a vast biplane machine, with a wing area of 4,000 sq. ft. and two 180 h.p. steam engines of his own lightweight design. Though this machine had two 18 ft. propellers, it was not intended that it should fly freely. It ran on rails, and on test it just rose from them, but was prevented from flying further by a set of check-rails. Since its weight was $3\frac{1}{2}$ tons it is remarkable that it managed to do even this before it crashed. Maxim experimented no more with flying till

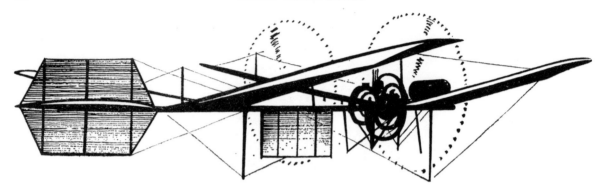

6. *Langley's 'Aerodrome', 1901. This tandem wing monoplane was driven by Manly's five-cylinder radial engine of 52 h.p. It came close to being the first powered heavier-than-air machine to achieve sustained flight*

1910, when he built a biplane which never got off the ground.

Many of the early experimenters, who all did their bit towards flying, have not been mentioned, but there was one more, who almost succeeded before the Wright brothers managed to take to the air in powered flight. He was an astronomer, S. P. Langley, the secretary of the Smithsonian Institution, which was founded by an Englishman in America. Langley studied the problems of flying, got the United States government interested, and produced a petrol engined model in 1901. This flew, and was thus the first petrol-engined model to do so. Encouraged by this success, Langley produced a full sized machine of 52 h.p. This was tested from a floating take-off vessel on the river Potomac in 1903. On two flights the machine fouled the launching catapult and fell into the river. The U.S. government, who had helped to pay for the experiments, lost interest. Nothing further was done, though the Smithsonian Institution continued to help and encourage flying in all its forms, as it still does today.

Langley only missed by nine days the chance of being the first man to fly a full size powered aeroplane. His last experiment was on December 8 1903. By 17 December the Wrights had flown their first powered aeroplane.

CHAPTER 2

The Age of Flying has Come

THE BROTHERS Wilbur (1867–1912) and Orville Wright (1871–1948) were bicycle sellers and manufacturers of Dayton, Ohio, U.S.A. From their business they paid for their flying experiments, calling their aeroplanes 'Flyers', the name which they had given to their bicycles.

They set about making an aeroplane that would fly in a scientific manner. Like solving a problem in geometry, they went from step to step in a logical way. Wilbur wrote to the Smithsonian Institution in May 1899 asking for copies of everything that had been written on flying. A large amount of literature on the subject was sent, including Langley's own writings on flying. A German, Otto Lilienthal (1848–96), had made considerable progress with gliding experiments. So also had the English engineer, Percy S. Pilcher (1866–99). He was the first British aviator, flying in a glider in 1895. The Wrights studied the work of these and other pioneers, whose experiments influenced the line of work on which they were busy. Octave Chanute (1832–1910), an American engineer, had collected all the information then available on flying. This, and his practical work on gliding, was also carefully studied.

Having read all this information, and thought over the whole subject, the Wrights decided to tackle the problem of flight in two stages. First they designed a glider, which was ready for use by September 1900. They took it to some lonely sand dunes at Kitty Hawk, North Carolina, having found that this spot on the Atlantic coast had strong and constant winds.

Though they made a few piloted glides in this 17-ft. span biplane, they flew it mostly as a kite, controlling it from the ground by cables. They were trying to prove that such a machine could be made to bank and turn by twisting the actual wings themselves, and thus be made to alter course and height. This method of control, which may now seem curious, was known as 'wing warping'. The Wrights later used it on all their early aeroplanes. It is still occasionally used on gliders today.

They found that this wing-twisting control would work satisfactorily. They therefore built a second biplane glider and took it to the Kill Devil Hills, near Kitty Hawk, in the summer of 1901. Here they set up a camp and started on piloted flight.

This camp, on a narrow sandbar separating Albemarle Sound from the Atlantic Ocean, was soon to become famous. It was four miles south of Kitty Hawk. In July 1901 a tent and a workshop, 16 × 25 × 6½ ft., were constructed.

The original workshop was a pretty flimsy affair, the roof covered with tarred paper to keep out the rain. In it the second biplane glider was put together and protected from the weather. It was, in effect, one of the world's first aircraft hangars. Like its many successors, it had large doors at each end, hinged at the top, one such door having a wicket. The doors could be propped open and held up horizontally. To add strength the sides of the building were buttressed outside with lean-to timbers. The tent, then forming the living quarters, was pitched alongside.

This little camp was not built without much labour and discomfort, and throughout its history was constantly in need of repairs and general first aid. The brothers arrived at Kill Devil in a storm of rain and wind, after a comfortless night spent with friends at Kitty Hawk. The tent was pitched with difficulty, and it was decided to bore a well. There was no fresh water within a mile of the camp. Unhappily the point of the drill was lost in the sand soon after work started, and they were eventually forced to catch water in a dishpan as the rain ran from the roof of the tent. Since the fabric of the tent had been treated with soap, the taste of the water must have been pretty horrible.

That was a Saturday, and on the Sunday night Orville was ill: hardly to be wondered at. By Monday he was up again, helping to build the 'hanger'. Things went fairly well till the Thursday, when the camp lay in the path of a swarm of mosquitos. Attacked by this ravenous horde, the brothers tried to escape them by wrapping themselves completely in blankets. Then the wind dropped, and the heat inside the blankets became unbearable. As soon as they emerged for a moment they were attacked again. On the Friday morning they attempted to begin work on the glider, but eventually had to give up the attempt, or be bitten to death. Already they were covered with irritating swellings from the bites they had received.

They rigged up mosquito nets for the next night, but so great was the swarm that these eventually proved of little help. Blankets were tried again, but eventually the campers resorted to the building of fires, using old tree trunks as fuel. They then tried to get some rest by sleeping in the track of the smoke. The camping party on this occasion, in addition to the brothers, consisted of E. C. Huffaker, an aeronautical investigator em-

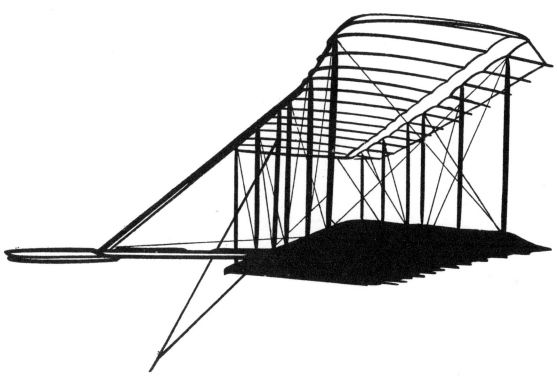

*7. The Wright brothers take the first step. Glider
no. 1, being flown as a kite at Kitty Hawk, 1900.
It was controlled from the ground by ropes*

ployed by Chanute, and Dr. G. A. Spratt, also an experimenter.

For the 1902 flying season the timber building was enlarged. During the time it had been standing the wind had blown the sand away from it, letting both ends drop two feet. Two days were spent in raising the building to its original level. The flimsy structure had 'paid off', since it bent, but did not break up.

Posts were now put in for the extension of the building, so that some living quarters could be provided in something less fragile than a tent. On 3 September some foundations and the floor were laid down, the frame being assembled on 4 September, and the tar papering went on the roof during 5 September. On the 6th the kitchen was moved in, and bunks were built high up under the roof. A picture of the kitchen shows it as an orderly arranged corner; with pots and pans hanging on the unplaned wooden walls, and a goodly array of tinned foods stacked on the shelves.

The camp building was now reasonably habitable, and would have delighted any schoolboy as a den. In another corner was the 'living room', with a stove, of which more in a moment, in the middle. The building had now been made sand and rain proof; the bunks were more comfortable than the cots they replaced, and a new well had been dug, giving a supply of good, clean water.

Transport consisted of a bicycle, no doubt of

8. ORVILLE WRIGHT (1871–1948)   *The first man in the world to fly a powered aeroplane in true flight, at 10.30 a.m., 17 December 1903*

Wright make, which travelled better on the sand than they had expected. A round trip from Kill Devil to Kitty Hawk, the nearest contact with civilisation, now only took an hour. This year, too, there was no swarm of mosquitos, so work progressed in more comfortable conditions, and it was now possible, with the use of the original cots, to sleep four.

The remoteness of the camp can be gleaned from a letter from Wilbur Wright to Chanute, telling him to come to the camp when convenient. 'A train leaves Norfolk' (Virginia) 'about 3 o'clock each day which connects with a steamer at Eliz-(abeth) City going to Roanoke Island,' he writes.

'A hack transfers passengers to Manteo, where you can spend the night. We will send a sailboat to meet you at Manteo and bring you to camp but must have notice of time of your coming. A telegram to me from Norfolk would probably be sufficient, though a previous notice, by mail, of the probable time would be better.' He goes on to advise warm clothes and blankets, and some heavy canvas or sailcloth for making additional cots. Remote as was the camp, it seems it could be reached by telegraph, over a line serving the Kill Devil Life Saving Station. Letters, no doubt, had to be collected from Kitty Hawk.

When the brothers arrived at camp on 25 September 1903, they found that the building had been blown from its foundation posts in a storm in the previous February. So, on 26th they began the foundations for a new building, to be 44 × 16 × 9 ft. By 2 October the roof was on, and the door ready for the north end. A storm struck the camp on October 18. As Wilbur wrote, 'The first night the wind was probably about 50 miles (p.h.) and Orville and I lost much sleep. . . . As the new building was not quite complete as to bracing, &c., we expected it to go first, so we lay there rocking on the billows waiting to hear it crash. Towards morning we could hear the water sloshing around on the floor of our old building, technically called the "summer house", the new building being called the "hand car", a corrup-

tion of the French "*hangar*" used by foreign airship men. Orville got up to investigate . . . and reported the floor under water at the north end, but the south end embracing the kitchen, library, &c. still dry.'

Then followed a battle in a 75 m.p.h. gale to keep the roof on. Fortunately the brothers succeeded in saving the building, getting soaked and buffeted in the process. By the end of the storm the damage was not too great.

The primitive heating stove mentioned was made out of a carbide can. When first lighted it smoked so badly that everything got covered with soot. This dropped from the roof into the plates at meal times. However, ingenious as ever, the

9. WILBUR WRIGHT (1867–1912) *The second man similarly to fly, later in the same morning in 1903. Died of typhoid fever*

brothers altered the stove, adding a different chimney, legs, and a number of dampers of their own invention so that, 'now we have about as good control in our stove as we have in our machine'. Various other improvements were made from time to time, such as the addition of a window in the south-east corner.

General conditions in the camp were by no means ideal for engineering work. Everything arrived by sea, and there was no landing stage within a mile of the camp. Supplies had to be hauled from a boat that put in to shore about two miles away.

The reason for the siting of the camp in this lonely spot, apart from the wind conditions already mentioned, was the presence of sand hills. These were constantly changing in height and slope, according to the direction and force of the winds. The absence of trees and the flat sandy surroundings were just what was needed, provided the disadvantages such as we have seen could be put up with.

Three sandhills were selected for the experiments. They were known as Big Hill, 100 ft high, Little Hill, 30 ft., and West Hill, 60 ft. In accordance with their custom of proceeding cautiously, Little Hill was used in the first experiments, and it was here that the first glider was flown as a kite.

It was at this camp, constantly torn by winter gales, at times infested by mosquitos, and always stark and bleak, that the brothers mounted their second glider, and prepared to learn to fly.

The pilot lay flat on the lower wing, with the cables which worked the wing-twisting in his hands. Two men ran with the glider till it took off. The brothers made alterations to the glider as their experience grew, and finally were able to fly up to distances of 389 ft. in wind speeds of 27 m.p.h.

But by the end of this flying season the Wrights were not satisfied with the results of their work. They had begun to see that much of what they had been reading was not true. They realised that they must find out from their own experiments how flying was to be made a success. So from September 1901 till August 1902 they concentrated on research work, based on their own ideas and experiments.

The Aeronautical Society of Great Britain had built a wind tunnel in 1871 for the purpose of experiment, and the Wrights built a similar tunnel and tested model gliders in it. The results obtained from these and many other experiments began to convince them that they were making some real progress. Based on their year's work they now built a third glider, and were back at their camp with it in December 1902.

The most obvious difference between this new glider and those which they had built before was

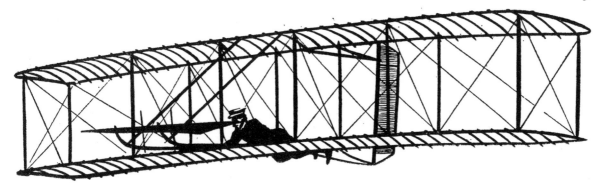

10. On the way to success. Wright's glider no. 3 at Kill Devil Hills, 1902

that the new machine was not just a pair of wings, one above the other. The new glider had an elevator, like a small movable wing, out in front, and a fixed double fin or tail out behind. Even so this new, 32-ft. span biplane proved to need some alterations, mainly the alteration of the double tail fin to a single hinged rudder. The cables which worked this rudder were joined to those which twisted the wings, and it was found that this allowed the machine to make smooth, banked turns. The Wrights therefore applied for a patent to protect this discovery, and later used this method of control for some years on a series of aeroplanes.

The results of their work with the modified glider No. 3 were considered to be satisfactory. Glides of up to 627 ft. were made, in wind speeds of up to 35 m.p.h. They found that the glider was under the full control of the pilot, and would bank and turn, rise and fall in response to the working of the control wires.

The brothers now felt that they had built an airframe into which they could put a motor and propellers, and that when this had been done the machine would not only fly, but could be controlled when in flight. The first part of the problem of powered flight had been solved.

There were a number of motor car engines available in 1902. Having examined them, the Wrights found that none of them were suitable for their purpose. They therefore designed their own engine, and helped to build it. The result was a 4-cylinder, 12 h.p. petrol engine, watercooled, which weighed, with fuel and water, only 200 lbs. The small petrol tank was hung on one of the forward wing struts, and the petrol ran by gravity to the carburettor, which passed the mixture of air and petrol to spring loaded automatic inlet valves. The exhaust valves were worked by a cam-shaft, very much as such valves are worked today, and the spark was provided by low tension magneto, driven from the flywheel.

The cooling system consisted of a long, thin tank of water, mounted vertically on another forward wing strut, and it roughly balanced the weight of the fuel tank, which was on the opposite side of the central line of the machine. The engine itself lay on its side on the lower wing. Its weight was about balanced by the pilot, who also lay flat on the lower wing, on the opposite side of the centre line. The engine drove two pusher propellers by bicycle chains. By crossing one of these chains in the form of a figure 8 it was arranged that these propellers revolved in opposite directions. Had this not been done the aeroplane would have 'pulled' in the direction in which both propellers turned. As it was, this 'twist' was cancelled out. Once it had been started, the speed of the engine could not be altered during flight. There was no throttle, such as is found on modern petrol engined machines.

This power unit was built into a biplane, with a wing span of 40 ft. 4 ins., and a wing area of 510 sq. ft. The main frames were of wood, the wings being made of a canvas-like material. There was a forward elevator out in front, to make the machine travel upwards or downwards, and a rear rudder fin behind, to make the machine turn. The whole aeroplane was mounted on skids, rather like a toboggan, and rollers were fitted so that the machine would run on the launching monorail. In fact these rollers appear to have been bicycle wheel hubs. The whole machine was braced together with wires. The pilot lay flat, balancing the weight of the engine, and worked the controls which operated the combined wing warping and rudder by means of a cradle in which his hips rested. In his left hand was the control lever which worked the forward elevator.

With this machine, Flyer number 1, the brothers returned to their camp at Kill Devil Hills in late September 1903. Here they found that their 1902 glider had been damaged. While repairing it they fitted a new rudder, similar to that fitted to Flyer number 1. They then practised flying with this glider before risking the Flyer in the air.

They ran into a little trouble with the Flyer, and several weeks were spent in repairs and slight alterations. The weather also held up the first attempt to fly, which had to be postponed from 12 December to 14 December.

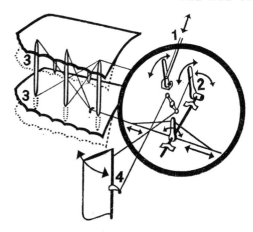

11. Control by wing-warping.

(1) Elevator lever,

(2) right hand lever rocked laterally to warp wings,

(3) and backwards and forwards to operate rudder (4)

On this day all was ready for the attempt. The 60-ft. launching monorail was laid downhill to help in acceleration, and the machine was placed with its rollers on the rail. A camera was fixed on a tripod to take pictures of the take-off, and witnesses were there to see the historic event. They came from the near-by Kill Devil Life Saving Station. The brothers tossed a coin for the honour of 'first flight', and the engine was started up. Wilbur won the toss, settled himself in the machine and opened up the engine. The check-wire was released, and the Flyer started down the rail. At the moment of take-off, Wilbur turned the front elevator up too far, anxious, in the excitement of the moment, that the machine should rise into the air. It rose steeply, stalled, and fell back, ploughing into the sand. Fortunately the damage caused was only slight. Repairs took some little time, during which the weather changed, and no further attempts to fly could be made till 17 December.

In the early morning of 17 December 1903, preparations for a flight were begun. This time the launching rail was laid on level ground. The camera was set up again, and the witnesses arrived from the Life Saving Station. Orville got into the machine. The engine was started up, and at 10.35 a.m. the check-wire was released. The Flyer ran about 40 ft. along the rail, rose into the air, and flew for about 12 seconds. It landed safely, 120 ft. from the point of take-off, and had travelled about 30 m.p.h.

The definition of this first powered flight, in the words of Orville Wright, is that the flight was 'the first in the history of the world in which a machine carrying a man had raised itself by its own power into the air in full flight, had sailed forward without reduction of speed, and finally landed at a point as high as that from which it started'. All other known claims to be the first man-carrying powered flight have been examined in the light of this definition, with the result that the claim of the Wright brothers has been found to be quite correct and justified.

For them this was their day of triumph. Whatever might follow, they had been the first to build a machine that would carry a man and fly under its own power. They made three more flights during the day, taking turns at the controls. Each time the distance flown increased. The fourth and final flight of the day lasted 59 seconds, and covered 852 ft, though the actual distance travelled through the air was just over half a mile. On landing from this flight, slight damage was caused to the elevator, so it was decided to end flying for the day. Unhappily, after the machine had been carried back to the camp a gust of wind overturned it, and it was wrecked. The brothers returned home to Dayton knowing that, after 4½ years of experimental work 'the age of flying,' as Orville said, 'had come at last'.

Satisfied with their work so far, the brothers began on their second powered machine, Flyer number 2. Meantime a Dayton banker, Torrence Huffman, had become interested in their experiments. He lent them a 90 acre field, known as Huffman Prairie. Here, 8 miles outside Dayton, the world's first aerodrome was established in 1904, and here, in May, the tests with Flyer number 2 were started.

Flyer number 2 was much the same as the first machine. A new, 15–16 h.p. motor was built for it. This motor was very similar to the first engine, but the cooling system now consisted of a number of vertical copper tubes, still fixed to one of the upright wing struts. This cooling system was more efficient, since the air could blow all round the tubes, the cooling area being very much increased. Tests were carried out over many weeks, during which 105 flights were made. These were kept short and low in altitude, partly on account of the size of the 90 acre field and partly because, in September, the brothers started to use a method of assisted take-off. This they used with all their aeroplanes till 1910, and they were anxious to become quite used to it.

This method of assisted take-off was quite simple. It consisted of a tall derrick of poles, inside which a weight, which could be altered as

12. [*opposite*]
The moment that was to change the world. The first powered sustained flight of a heavier-than-air machine. Orville Wright becomes airborne, 17 December 1903, at Kill Devil Hills, U.S.A. Wilbur, who by bad luck had crashed on his attempt on 14 December is seen running, on the left. The official photographer snaps the take-off and the official witnesses from the Kill Devil Life Saving Station look on

necessary, was hung by a rope. The rope passed over a pulley and ran down to the launching rail at the starting end. It then ran along to the take-off end, and back once more to the truck on which the aeroplane rested. When the weight was released it descended inside the poles, hauling in the rope as it fell. The rope drew the truck with the aeroplane resting on it, with its engine running, along the launching rail. As soon as sufficient speed had been reached, through the combined efforts of the weight and the engine, the aeroplane took off.

The progress of the Wrights' experiments was now steady and continuous. During the 1904 flying season they made the first circular flight, and the first flight of over five minutes. By the 1905 flying season they had designed Flyer number 3, which was ready for use in June. It had the same engine as Flyer number 2, but this was now rated at 15–21 h.p., its power having increased with use. The airframe included further improvements gained by previous experience.

Flyer number 3 had a 40 ft. 6 in. wing span, a wing area of 503 sq. ft., was 28 ft. long, stood 9 ft. 5⅛ in. high, and weighed 710 lb. without fuel and water. As before, it was mounted on skids. By October this machine had flown a distance of 24⅕ miles in one flight, the distance travelled being only limited by the amount of petrol carried. During this season of flying the wing-twisting and rudder wires were made into separate controls. Flyer number 3 was used again in 1908, and by this time the pilot had been provided with a seat. During the three years in between quite a lot had been happening in the experimental world of flying.

CHAPTER 3

Europe Takes a Hand

IT MAY SEEM odd that, with so much achieved and with so much more to be done, the Wrights disappeared from the picture from 1905 till 1908. But they knew what they were doing, and we shall see that, when they staged their 'come-back' it was well timed, and with dramatic effect. One of their reasons for apparent retirement was that they had no wish that all which they had done should be 'pirated' by other experimenters. The story of discovery is strewn with the names of men who, having made important progress, and having a fortune in their grasp, died penniless, while others grew fat on their work. The Wrights had no intention of falling into this trap.

They had applied for a patent to protect one of their inventions, the combined control system, and it was some years before this was granted. They offered the results of their work to the governments of the U.S.A., Britain, and France in turn. For various reasons none of these governments took advantage of the offer at that time, though each of them had begun to see the possible military use for the aeroplane.

While the Wrights were out of the public eye, a number of experimenters in Europe pressed on with their flying experiments. None of them had official help. They spent their own money on their experiments, and sometimes their own lives as well. We have already said that the American engineer, Chanute, himself keenly interested in flying, made it his business to collect all the information he could find on the flying experiments going on, including the work of the Wrights. He now came over to Europe, met those who were experimenting with flight, and gave some lectures on the whole subject.

As a result the European experimenters thought that they now held in their hands the secrets of the Wrights' success, and that they could copy their work. But Chanute did not know everything about the Wrights' work. As a result, the Europeans who tried to copy them mainly met with failure. This made them think that the claims of the Wrights had been exaggerated: that the Wrights were wrong. Just as the Wrights had found that much of what they had read in the early days of their

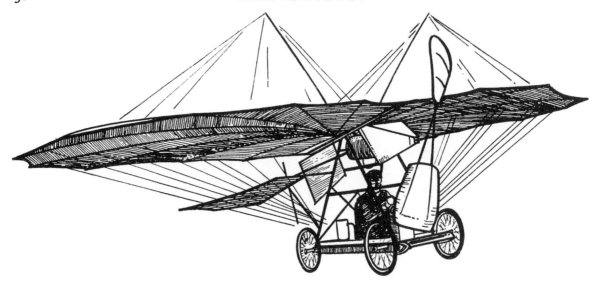

13. The Vuia monoplane of 1906, which was to influence European monoplane design. It was the first aeroplane to be mounted on pneumatic tyres

experiments was incorrect, so the European experimenters found that what they had been told about the Wrights' work was incomplete, and only led them to failure. So they continued to work on flying, following their own ideas, often with little success. But even so, progress was being made.

A series of engines, known as the Antoinettes, were built in France, and were suitable for use in aeroplanes, being designed for the purpose. A small aeroplane factory was opened at Billancourt. But it was not till 1906 that Vuia, a Hungarian living in Paris, built the first full-size monoplane which began to look something like the aeroplanes we now know.

This little machine was powered by a carbonic acid gas engine, and had an undercarriage that looked like a flat cart, mounted on four wheels, on which the pilot sat. It had pneumatic tyres, and was the first aeroplane ever to do so. It never really flew, but is credited with considerable influence on the aircraft designs of the future. It is said to have influenced Blèriot in his work. This was the man who was to be the first to fly the English Channel. That he did so was, perhaps, more by luck than judgement, as we shall presently see.

At the time the Vuia monoplane was built, Blèriot was experimenting with biplanes, to which he was to return in time to come. The Vuia design, however, started him working on monoplanes, and in one such craft he made his historic flight. But at first his experiments with monoplanes were not all

14. Santos–Dumont flying his 14-bis. This machine made the first official aeroplane flights in Europe in 1906. It was so numbered because it was first tested slung beneath his dirigible airship no. 14

15. LOUIS BLÈRIOT   *One of the greatest and most successful French pioneers. Originally an engineer. Famous always as the man who, more by luck than judgement, flew the English Channel*

successful. His Canard (1903) only 'hopped', and in his Libellule he was nearly killed. But he was on the right road, and was soon to achieve success.

Meantime Santos-Dumont, who had carried out a great deal of work on airships, now turned his attention to heavier-than-air machines. In 1906–7 he produced his 'Demoiselle'. This was a remarkable light aeroplane, weighing only 243 lb. complete with its two-cylinder engine. It was controlled in flight by two rudders and a forward elevator. As well as being the first man to fly an airship round the Eiffel Tower, Santos-Dumont is credited with the first powered heavier-than-air

flight in Europe. This flight he made in a box-kite-like machine, powered by a 50-h.p. Antoinette petrol engine. In September 1906 he piloted this machine on a flight of 197 ft., to win a prize of 3,000 French francs.

It will be seen, then, that, in spite of many failures, considerable progress was being made by the flyers in Europe before the Wrights came over and changed the whole picture. During the first

16. ALBERT SANTOS-DUMONT *Brazilian pioneer, working in France. Built many successful lighter-than-air machines and dirigibles. Flew no. 6 dirigible round the Eiffel Tower, 1901. Built his first aeroplane 1906, the 14-bis (illustration p. 31). Famous for his light aircraft, the Demoiselle series*

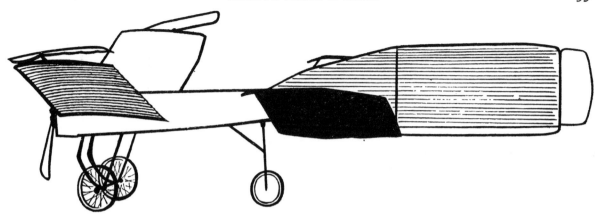

17. *The Blèriot VI, 1907, the tandem wing Libellule (Dragonfly). Compare Langley's tandem wing Aerodrome of 1901 (p. 16). The best flight of the Libellule, after alteration, was of 603½ feet in September 1907*

half of 1908 the Englishman, Henry Farman, flying in France, won a prize for a circuit of one mile. In May the same man took up the first passenger to fly in Europe, when he carried his fellow experimenter, Ernest Archdeacon. Only a few days before Wilbur Wright, now back in the air, had taken up the world's first aerial passenger, C. W. Furnas, in a flight in the U.S.A. In July another experimenter took up the first woman passenger Madame Peltier, over Turin in Italy. This lady was also to become the world's first woman to fly solo.

In England S. F. Cody, an American showman later to become naturalised, produced his 'British

c

Army Aeroplane No. 1', at Farnborough in 1908. Not a great deal of the details of this machine appear to be still known. It was a biplane, based on Wright construction. In October 1908, it completed a flight of 1,390 ft. Though it then crashed, Cody pressed on, continued to build, and by 1909 was taking up passengers. As far as can be seen from a model in the Science Museum, this aeroplane had a wing span of 52 ft., and a length of 36 ft. It was powered by a water-cooled, 50 h.p. V8 Antoinette engine, the radiator being a system

18. *Voisin–Delagrange powered biplane of 1907, making a hop-flight. This machine used the first fixed fins in combination with a rudder. The fins were the vertical sides of the box-kite type tail units, the rudder being mounted between the horizontal planes*

of vertical tubes, mounted between the wings, very like the cooling system on the Wright Flyer number 2. The engine drove, by chains, two pusher propellers, which were mounted between the actual wings of the aircraft. It had a large rudder at the rear, pivoted top and bottom, and a small rudder mounted on top of the higher wing. It was well supplied with wheels, to meet any eventuality of rock-and-roll. The main landing wheels were below the body of the machine, with a smaller wheel out in front, giving a type of tricycle under-carriage. The tail was supported by another wheel, and to counter excessive roll, there was a wheel at

each end of the lower wing. Built mainly of wood and canvas, the wing area was 880 sq. ft. and the total weight of the aeroplane, without fuel and water, was about 1 ton.

A difference of opinion now arose as to who was the first Briton to fly a powered aeroplane in Britain. Cody had not become naturalised when he took up his 'British Army Aeroplane No 1'. A. V. Roe, later to give his name to Avro, built an aeroplane which flew at Brooklands in 1906. This machine did not take off under its own power, but was towed into the air by a car, much as some gliders are now towed into the air by a mechanical winch. It has now been settled that the first Briton to fly a powered aeroplane in Britain was J. T. C. Moore-Brabazon, then a very young man, later

20. L. DELAGRANGE *A sculptor turned aviator, 'The field of practical aviation' (in Europe) '— in the all-important years from 1902 to 1908—was abandoned to the enthusiastic efforts of a few rich amateurs' (GIBBS-SMITH). Of these Delagrange was one*

19. S. F. CODY *Cowboy, marksman, and theatrical showman, an American, later naturalised, and a life-long flying enthusiast. The first man in Britain to take up a passenger, Col. J. E. Capper, Commanding Officer at Farnborough, on 16 August 1909. Later the same day took up Mrs. Capper, thereby earning her the distinction of being the first British woman to fly in Britain*

Lord Brabazon of Tara, holder of British pilot's licence No. 1, and the 'grand old man' of British aviation (1884–1963), whose motor car bore the distinctive registration number, FLY 1.

In the U.S.A. too, work was progressing. Bell, Curtiss, Selfridge, and many others were building aircraft, one of which, in June 1908, flew 6,000 ft. at 39 m.p.h.

While all this had been going on the Wrights, though apparently 'chair-borne', were actually

21. British Army Aeroplane no. 3, 1910

hard at work. During 1906 and 1907 they had been building greatly improved engines. Satisfied that their airframe and its controls were suitable, they were concentrating on the power-pack that was to drive it. They had also been hammering at the U.S. and French governments, and in 1908 made an official 'acceptance test,' which will be mentioned later, to the satisfaction of the U.S. authorities. They also succeeded in reaching an agreement to have their aeroplanes built in France.

In preparation for all that was to come, they took their 1905 aeroplane back to Kill Devil Hills, modified it to take both pilot and passenger sitting upright, and in May 1908, Wilbur took up C. W. Furnas, as previously recorded. This is anticipat-

ing events a little since, in 1907, in the hope of an agreement with France, they had finalised a two-seater aeroplane and shipped it to the Continent.

This machine had a wing span of 41 ft., with a total wing area of about 510 sq. ft. It weighed 800 lbs. without fuel and water, and was powered by a 30–40 h.p., 4-cylinder engine, which was now set vertically in the airframe. Its length was 31 ft. and its speed 35–40 m.p.h., and like all the Wright aeroplanes it was mounted on skids. During this period somewhat similar aeroplanes were built in England by Shorts, and in France, under 'licence' from the Wrights.

It was now the moment for the Wrights to break into the European flying scene. Wilbur, who had come over to Europe, got the 1907 aeroplane out of the warehouse at Le Havre, where it had languished for some months. The long journey from Dayton and the period of storage had taken its toll of what was, after all, a flimsy machine of little more than wood and canvas. Awaiting the much publicised flight of the Wright aeroplane, the public grew impatient. May faded into June: June into July, and still the machine remained grounded.

At last, on 8 August 1908, Wilbur made his first flight from European soil. By the 17th he had made 9 further flights, the longest of over 8 minutes. The centre of operations was then moved from Le Mans to the military grounds at Camp

d'Auvours, a few miles away, and the successful flights continued. Before the end of 1908 over 100 had been made. During the series Wilbur remained aloft for some 26 hours, breaking every record then existing for a powered aeroplane flight. Sixty flights were made with passengers. In September he covered 41 miles in just over 90 minutes, an endurance record. In October he took

22. The Blèriot VII, 1907. A low-wing tractor monoplane of prophetic configuration. The enclosed fuselage was somewhat in advance of current design. Powered by a 50 h.p. Antoinette engine, the machine flew first in November, its best flight being 1,640 feet. After several good short flights and turns it crashed on landing on 18 December and was abandoned. With only a rudder and elevons to form the tail unit, it was of the inherently unstable design. (Elevon = a control surface combining the functions of elevator and aileron)

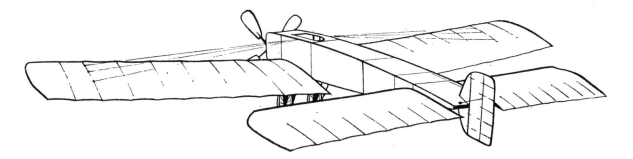

up a passenger for the then longest passenger flight of 1 hour 9 minutes, covering 45 miles. In December he covered 77 miles in 2 hours 20 minutes and won a prize of 20,000 French francs. Finally, in December, he broke all the then altitude records on the 18th by reaching a height of 360 ft., just over one third of the height of the Eiffel Tower. Thus, by practical demonstration, Wilbur Wright showed that the Wright aeroplanes could do all or better than had been claimed.

Orville Wright had not been idle while his brother was carrying out the 'air conquest' of Europe. He had been flying the army acceptance tests, already mentioned, at Fort Myer. He had also taken up passengers. With one of these, Lt.

23. The Blèriot V of 1907, of the canard type. The French word 'canard' meaning duck; was applied to the type of aeroplane that flew 'tail first', with the fuselage and elevator forward of the main wings. Powered by a 24 h.p. Antoinette motor the best 'hop' of the Blèriot V was 20 feet

T. E. Selfridge, he was unfortunate enough to crash, his passenger being killed. Selfridge thus gained the sad distinction of being the first air passenger so to die. The crash was caused by what would now be known as 'material fatigue'.

So, with reasonable accuracy, it can be said that, both in Europe and the U.S.A., the example of the Wrights stimulated many others, and encouraged them to continue working towards increased efficiency and greater efforts at the conquest of the air.

CHAPTER 4

Progress and Achievement

AT THIS PERIOD France became the centre of aeronautical affairs in Europe. Here many were at work, building and developing better aeroplanes, and finer engines to drive them. Now they had before them the example of the Wrights, at a zenith from which they were about to decline.

Noteworthy among the experimenters was Blèriot, who had been building and developing his machines for some years. Competition now arose between Blèriot and Hubert Latham for the honour of being the first to fly the English Channel. An oversea flight of this magnitude, from which there was 'no return', had not so far been attempted.

The attempt was made in 1909 when, on 19 July Latham set out from Calais in his Antoinette. Eight miles out his engine failed, and he came down in the sea. Ten days later he tried again, and was again brought down when only one mile from the English coast.

Blèriot made his attempt in his aeroplane mark XI, which he had been developing for some time. He set out from France in this light mono-plane on 25 July. Powered by a 25 h.p. motor, and controlled by wing warping and rudder, he got his aeroplane across, to win a prize of £1,000, and orders for 100 or more such aircraft. His famous mark XI became a standard aeroplane which, with various modifications, was used till about 1914. It had a forward 3 cylinder engine and twin-bladed propeller. The engine was mounted in a square-section tapering fuselage, the wasp-like wings being fixed across the top. These were held firm from below by wires connected to the wheeled undercarriage, while above, a king-post structure placed centrally along the wings, had wires fixed to it which exerted an upward pull on the wings at various points. Behind the pilot the fuselage was left open, and the tail unit was kept clear of the ground by a skid. The front wheels were on a rather long supporting framework, which made the whole machine appear to stand rather high off the ground. After all the odd shapes and types that had appeared in the past the Blèriot mark XI looked a capable and airworthy machine.

Its competitor for the Channel honours, Lath-

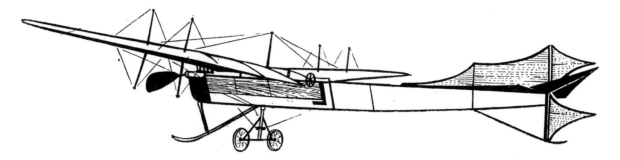

24. The 'Antoinette IV'. It flew first in October 1908 and was the first of Levavasseur's true Antoinette monoplanes. In this machine Latham tried to cross the Channel on 9 July 1909. His second attempt was in 'Antoinette VII' on 27 July. Unhappily, both attempts failed

am's Antoinette, was a more rakish-looking machine. The square-section fuselage was long and slim, with the engine mounted at the front end and clearly visible above the framework. The square-ended, slightly tapered wings were mounted above the fuselage and behind the engine, the two wings being separate. They were held firm by five king posts and wires. The pilot sat in a shallow open cockpit behind them. The tail consisted of four parts at right-angles to each other, and the machine was supported on the ground by wheels and a skid, which stuck out in front. The aeroplane was said to be graceful in flight and capable of flying in rough weather.

During this period two important matters were gradually being ironed out. These were, for stable or unstable aircraft, and for wing warping control or ailerons. Throughout their experiments

the Wrights had always been in favour of an unstable aircraft that would not tend to right itself in the air, but was dependent upon the skill of the pilot. The European builders mainly constructed stable aircraft at and after this period. They did not entirely trust the instability of the Wright-type machines. Thus the Wrights and the unstable type of aircraft began to fade into the background.

Another vital point was also being gradually worked out, though this did not reach a final conclusion till well after the point at which our story

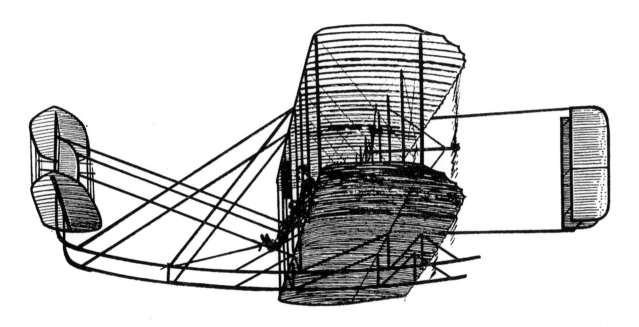

*25. Wilbur Wright's first flight in France, at Hunaudières
Race Course, near Le Mans, 8 August 1908*

finishes. This was the question of preference for monoplane or biplane machines. As will be seen, the latter looked like being established for all time. Even a triplane or two appeared from time to time, such as that built by A. V. Roe in 1909.

This machine consisted of a long fuselage, roughly square in section. On the front end were mounted three 'layers' of wings, the engine being

26. HUBERT LATHAM *Half-English, half-French, always flew Levavasseur's Antoinettes. Crossed the Golden Gate, San Francisco, in an Antoinette, February 1911. Made an unsuccessful attempt to fly the Channel ahead of Blèriot, on 9 July 1909 and a second similar attempt after Blèriot, on 29 July. Suffered engine failure on both attempts.*

placed between the lower and middle planes, some distance below the slim, four blade propeller. The tail unit also consisted of a triplane structure, and the pilot sat well back behind the wings. Braced with a mass of wires and struts and mounted on thin 'bicycle' wheels, the whole machine looked like some fantastic insect. The buzzing of its 9 h.p. two-cylinder motor-bicycle engine no doubt added to the illusion.

Blèriot was working on monoplanes at this time, though he was, a little later, to change his opinion about them. Both he and Latham had, as mentioned, used monoplanes, with wing warping, for their Channel attempts.

A great deal of the shape of aircraft to come was to be seen at Reims aviation week, held in August 1909. This was the first aeroplane meeting ever to be held. Though not all the types then being built were on show, a fairly representative selection appeared. While many of the leading aircraft designers and builders were there, the Wrights were not, though six machines of their design were included in the exhibition. In all, 38 machines were exhibited, of which 18 made flights.

At this moment Europe held a definite lead over U.S.A. in aircraft design and construction, but the Curtiss, an American aeroplane, won the speed contest at 43·3 m.p.h., even though Blèriot put up a speed record of 47·8. Wind and weather caused some postponements, but the meeting as a whole was of great importance. It formed an undoubted turning point in aviation history.

It is a pity that fuller details of the aircraft entered for this aviation week have failed to survive. This, in part, is due to the fact that not a few of them had alterations made during the actual meeting. An eyewitness of the flights made by the various machines remarks on the steadiness, by comparison, of the different types when

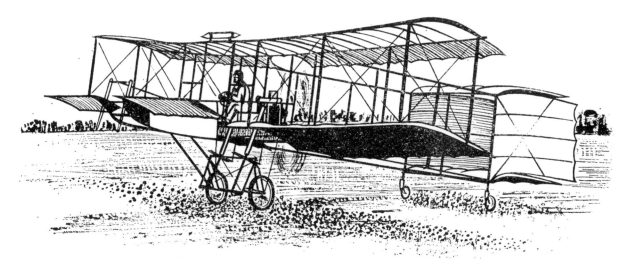

27. Delagrange flying the single-seat, 50 h.p. Voisin biplane of 1908-9

in the air, saying that the Wright machines seemed the least steady. Their aeroplanes were in the hands of experts, but the impression given by them when in flight was no doubt a further blow against them in the stable versus unstable type of design. Latham set up a height record of 508 ft., and Farman a distance record of 112 miles. Though four aircraft were wrecked during the .week, no one was killed. A Blèriot XII caught fire, the first aircraft in history to be so destroyed. A prize was given for passenger carrying. This

was won by an aeroplane which took up three people.

The European aircraft of 1909, as shown at the meeting, were mainly biplanes, with forward elevator, a pusher airscrew, and one or more rudders. It was not till 1911 that the front elevator largely disappeared and a tractor airscrew replaced the pusher to a large extent.

The monoplanes, however, bore more resemblance to the type of aircraft now familiar, having a long fuselage, tractor airscrew, ailerons or wing

28. GLEN CURTISS *American aircraft designer and engineer. A contemporary of the Wright brothers. Developed the seaplane and flying boat*

warping, and a tail unit. With the monoplane the Wrights never experimented, and as their influence began to wane, it was they who now followed the lead of others in such matters.

By the end of 1909 many types of engine were being built. Some had the cylinders in line, some in V formation. Some had the cylinders placed fan-wise, or in a circle, and the rotary engine made its appearance. These rotary engines were, to modern eyes, something quite remarkable. The whole engine, consisting of 3, 7 or 9 cylinders: always an odd number: revolved about a central shaft. As it revolved it actuated the overhead valve

push rods and the connecting rods and pistons. Working at a speed of about 1,300 revolutions per minute, it must have set up heavy strains on the aircraft frame. It was a successful engine for many years, but has long since become an engine of the past.

The rotary engine was for so many years the main power unit of early aircraft that some fuller details should be given about it. Its design arose, in part, from the constant search for a lightweight engine. The rotary engine scored in this respect because of the short length of its crankcase and crankshaft. All the piston rods met the crankshaft at almost the same point. The shaft was therefore short and its casing smaller than is the case with cylinders set in line, as on the Wright and other engines. Some of the disadvantages were that it used a lot of oil, and it had a certain gyroscopic effect on the airframe. While it was possible to make a tight turn in one direction, in the opposite direction it was sometimes necessary to climb while making the turn, owing to this gyroscopic

29. [opposite]
Spanning Britain's ancient moat. Louis Blèriot arrives over Dover, 25 July 1909. 'The day that Blèriot flew the Channel marked the end of our insular safety, and the beginning of the time when Britain must seek another form of defence beside her ships.' [SIR ALAN COBHAM]

effect of the engine, revolving like a flywheel. A few experiments with the popular gyroscopic top will illustrate this point.

The reason why the whole engine revolved was quite simple. The hollow crankshaft, which carried the main bearings for supporting the engine and taking the propeller thrust was fixed, so that the engine revolved round it. The same effect can be obtained if a toy electric motor is held by its driving shaft. When the current is turned on, the whole motor will revolve round its own shaft. A propeller mounted on the stationary shaft, but fixed to the motor body, will revolve as the motor turns.

The engines were made by two French firms which later amalgamated to form the Gnôme-et-Rhône Engine Company. Building of the Gnôme engines was begun by Louis Sequin in 1895, the company being founded in 1905. In 1911 M. Verdet was also producing a rotary engine, known as the Rhône, and the amalgamation took place at the beginning of World War I. The two makes of engine were much the same, and were improved as time went on.

As stated, the number of cylinders was always an odd number. The seven-cylinder engine developed into a fourteen cylinder and the nine into an eighteen, these multicylinder engines being, in effect, two engines, placed one behind the other. In later engines of this type the two sets of

30. ROBERT ESNAULT-PELTERIE *The able engineer who was one of the leaders of the Chanute-inspired campaign to revive European aviation*

cylinders were made to revolve in opposite directions.

The nickel-steel, air cooled cylinders were evenly spaced round a cylindrical steel crankcase. Each cylinder had one overhead exhaust valve, the inlet valve being incorporated in the top of the piston. A very simple carburettor, fed by gravity, sprayed the petrol into the hollow crankshaft. As the engine revolved and the piston travelled down the cylinder, the valve in the piston top opened and the petrol vapour passed through.

The upstroke of the piston closed the valve and compressed the vapour, which was exploded by a sparking plug, which received its spark from a magneto. The plug was usually placed on the leading side of the engine to help keep it cool. After the explosion of the petrol vapour the exhaust escaped into the atmosphere through the upper valve. This overhead exhaust valve produced the effect so often seen in films of early aeroplanes of a large amount of smoke pouring from the engine as it started up.

In later Gnôme engines, introduced in 1913, the piston-head inlet valve, which needed a certain amount of spring control, was replaced by a series of holes in the lower part of the inner cylinder wall. In this type of engine the exhaust valve on top remained open for a few moments as the piston descended, letting in the right amount of air above the piston. After it had closed the piston passed below the level of the inlet holes in the sides of the cylinder on its downward stroke. The petrol vapour, still fed into the crankcase,

31. Wright's 1907–9 type, a modified version of that in figure 25 on page 41.

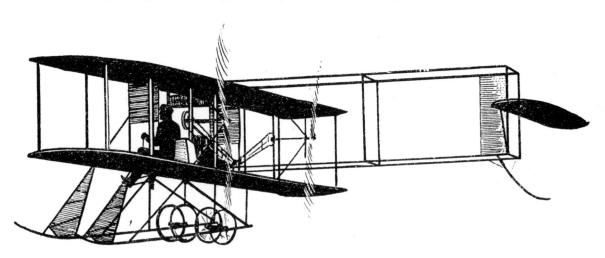

escaped through the holes into the cylinder above the piston. The upstroke compressed the air and petrol mixture, the plug sparked at the moment of highest compression, and the cycle was complete. This type was known as the Gnome Monosoupape, or single valve, engine. The revolving crankcase was also made to work the overhead exhaust valve, through gears and camwheels.

It was found that the air cooling was not always absolutely satisfactory, since the leading side of each cylinder ran cooler than the trailing side as it travelled first through the air. This caused the metal of the cylinder to expand unevenly through the great heat of the explosion within it. Special piston rings had to be evolved in order to keep

32. The Goupy tractor biplane no. II of 1909. Note the staggered wings and tailplane assembly. As built the machine had between-wing ailerons, fitted in front of the wings. These were changed late in the year to the pivoting wing-tip ailerons on the upper planes, as shown. The biplane tail unit had pivoted elevators on the tips of the lower planes, as shown, throughout. Behind this unit was the rudder

the piston gas-tight in what was a not-quite-round cylinder.

In order to keep the engine lubricated, their

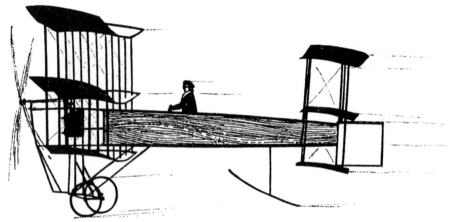

33. A. V. Roe, flying his first tractor triplane, 1909. Triplanes appeared from time to time, but were never very much favoured

being no sump of oil as in a stationary, in-line engine, oil was fed into the hollow crankshaft and so to the crankcase downstream of the carburettor. By entering the crankcase with the fuel the oil kept the bearings and various other internal parts lubricated. Much the same effect is obtained in motorcycles and scooter engines today by the use of 'two-stroke mixture', that is, oil and petrol combined, the mixture being put into the 'petrol tank'. In the rotary engine castor oil was used since, to a large extent, it will not dissolve in petrol, thereby losing its lubricating power.

One of the main differences between the Gnôme

D

and the Rhône engines was that the latter had both the inlet and exhaust valves on the top of the cylinders, like an overhead valve car engine. There were many other technical differences, but in the main both engines were very much the same.

Many of the great achievements of the rotary engined aeroplanes were made after the time when this story closes, but by 1910 Farman had achieved his 8½-hour endurance record with a 50 h.p. Gnôme engine. In the same year Blèriot put up a speed record of 67·5 m.p.h. in a biplane with a 100 h.p. Gnôme engine. Blèriot, Farman, Voisin, and many other of the early fliers used the rotary engine, to be followed by such famous aircraft firms as Bristol, Short, Avro, and Sopwith. In the age of the jet aircraft we are unlikely to see such engines again, but they probably contributed more than any other single factor to the success of the earlier powered fliers, and achieved great distinction during World War I.

Power varied from 25 to 100 h.p. At the turn of the year, Blèriot's record had not been surpassed, but Farman had flown $145\frac{1}{2}$ miles in one of Blèriot's aircraft, and Latham had been up 1,486 ft. in an Antoinette.

From now till the outbreak of World War I in 1914, flying steadily increased, and the whole picture broadened out very rapidly. Britain, so far lagging behind France in design and development, now began to gain ground. In America also, flying took on an increasing tempo.

As popular interest in flying grew, passenger carrying and 'joy riding' increased. To add to the increasing production of monoplanes and biplanes, the float-plane, father of the seaplane, made its appearance. The Wrights and their Flyers were still popular, but they were gradually being

34. The second type of Curtiss biplane of 1909

35. *Henri Farman's first individually designed biplane. It flew first in April 1909, and was called the Henri Farman III. It was to become one of the most popular European biplanes*

eclipsed. Even so it was in an aeroplane of the Wright type that the Hon. C. S. Rolls made a double, non-stop Channel crossing. At the Paris Salon exhibition of October 1910 a Coander biplane, built entirely of wood, was on show. It was powered by a 50 h.p. engine. This drove a fan, sucking in air and driving it backwards to form a jet. Though unsuccessful, this was the first full-size jet propelled aeroplane to be attempted.

In America, flights between towns, such as from Albany to New York, and New York to Phila-

delphia, began to be made. One American aviator, Eugene Ely, took off from an 87-ft. platform built on the cruiser *Birmingham*. Later the same pilot flew out to sea and landed on the cruiser *Pennsylvania*, took off again, and returned to base at San Francisco.

Geoffrey de Havilland, founder of the famous firm, now became designer at the government aircraft factory at Farnborough. Cody flew 185 miles in a circuit, and flying began in Spain, Switzerland, Argentine, Brazil, Saigon, Indo-China, and China itself. T. O. M. Sopwith took his pilot's licence at Brooklands. Olympia put on an aircraft show, and flying meetings began to be held all over Europe, including many places in Britain.

36. The Avro biplane of 1911. This machine, with other contemporary British types, is considered of importance in setting the style of tractor biplanes of the future. From it came the 504 (illustration no. 45). Powered by a 35 h.p. Green engine, this machine still used wing warping. This practice gave place to ailerons on the Avros of 1912. Note the high-mounted engine with radiator above and behind it, the double landing wheels, precursor of landing gear to come, and the landing skids

37. SIR GEOFFREY DE HAVILLAND *Came into the aviation picture in 1910, building and testing two biplanes. Still very much in the picture. Won highest marks piloting the B.E. 2, (illustration p. 59) at the first Military Aeroplane Competition, held at Larkhill, Salisbury Plain, in August 1912*

Radio communication between an aeroplane and the ground began to be tested, as did the dropping of bombs. Aerodromes were opened throughout Europe, among them such famous places as Brooklands and Hendon. Long distance flights continued to increase; as from Hendon to

38. The Short 'triple twin' of 1911, the first multi-engine aircraft to fly

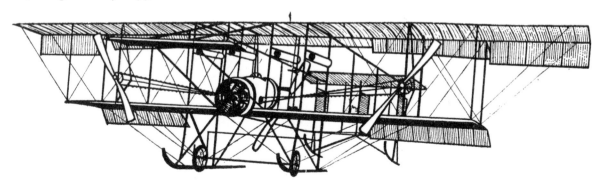

Paris, and St. Louis to New York. One remarkable flight was made in America by C. P. Rodgers. Followed by a special train-load of spare parts, he set out in 1911 to fly from New York to Long Beach, California, via Chicago and San Antonio, some 4,000 miles. His Wright biplane took 82 flying hours, spread over 82 stages, the total time taken being 49 days. He crashed 15 times, so that by the time he reached Long Beach, not much of his original aeroplane was left.

Aeroplanes were still settling into main types: pusher biplanes, tractor biplanes and tractor monoplanes. More metal was being used in con-struction, and a German monoplane was fitted with a primitive retractable undercarriage. Wing warping control was less and less used. Shorts produced what was claimed to be the first twin engined aeroplane in history, with two independent engines, driving three propellers. This was a quite remarkable machine. Known as the Short triple-twin, its upper wing was 40 feet long, the lower being 29 ft. It had both a front and rear engine. The forward engine drove two propellers, while that at the rear drove the third. The engines

39. The R.E.P. 2 by Esnault–Pelterie, 1908

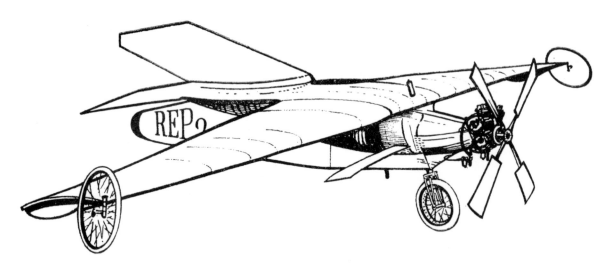

themselves were two 50 h.p. Gnome machines. The rear engine must have added a real 'boost' to the machine, connected to only one propeller, while the front engine drove its two propellers by chains, in the traditional Wright manner. The aeroplane as a whole was constructed of the traditional wood and canvas, had a length of 37 ft., and was mounted on wheels and skids. It had a large triple rudder and the pilot, seated between the wings, had an engine fore and aft.

Curtiss, in America, brought out the first practical seaplane in 1911, adapting his land aeroplane by placing a float underneath. He was soon to become a world leader in seaplane building.

The governments of the world began to worry about the possible uses of aeroplanes in war. Mr.

40. The Curtiss Flying Boat of 1913. Unlike the earlier Curtiss seaplane, 1911, the pilot and passenger now sit in the boat, instead of on the front of the lower wing. The boat has developed from a large float, which supported the earlier machine when on the water

Winston Churchill, as he then was, soon convinced himself of the importance of aircraft as weapons. In San Francisco the first tests were made with dropping live bombs, and these were quickly followed by the first bomb sight. Rifles and machine guns began to be carried. A start was made with flying mail by air, from Allahabad in India in February 1911, and from Hendon to

41. SIR A. V. ROE *Founder of the Avro company.*
Won second prize for his model aeroplane at
Alexandra Palace exhibition, April 1907. Tested a
full-size aeroplane based on this model at Brooklands,
1908. A controversial figure in the 'first Briton to
fly in Britain' claim. 'A brilliant man, and tributes
galore have been justifiably paid to him'

[GIBBS-SMITH]

Windsor in September, followed by similar flights
in the U.S.A. in the same and the following
month. The Wrights themselves had partially returned to gliding, Orville setting up a record of $9\frac{3}{4}$
minutes while testing an automatic stabiliser
during the last flying season ever to be held at
Kill Devil Hills. Obviously they were beginning
to take stability seriously.

By 1912 a new form of building was being introduced. Known as monocoque construction, it
consisted of building the fuselage of the aeroplane
in such a way that it carried most of the load. Till
now the fuselage had been mainly a light framework, often covered with canvas-like material,
used, more or less, to place the tail unit at a sufficient distance behind the main wings. Now the
fuselage became a strong structure, to develop as
the main passenger or freight carrying portion of
the aeroplane in time to come. An attempt was
also made to construct an aeroplane with alumi-
nium, and in France the first all-metal aeroplane
in history appeared, though it was not to prove a
really practical monoplane.

Curtiss now modified his 1911 float-plane or
flying-boat into a flying-boat proper. The central
float was enlarged to take the pilot, who no longer
sat up on the front of the lower wing. From this
and other experiments came a long line of Curtiss
flying-boats, one being launched at Washington
Navy Yard by a compressed-air-driven launcher.
Sufficient float-type aircraft were now being built

42. [*opposite*]
The father of the aircraft carriers of today. An
aircraft takes off from H.M.S. Hibernia *while*
under weigh, 1912

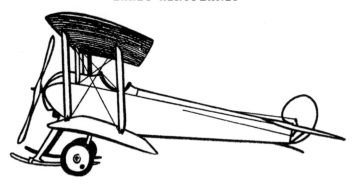

43. The Sopwith Tabloid of 1913. This 80 h.p., 92 m.p.h. light aeroplane did a great deal (with the B.E.2, which see) to revolutionise the biplane, and to kill for many years to come the further construction of monoplanes

for the first seaplane meeting to be held at Monaco in March. In another field of experiment, Lawrence Sperry built the first automatic pilot, which he successfully demonstrated on a Curtiss floatplane on Lake Keuke, New York State. Captain Albert Berry made the first parachute drop in March, at St. Louis, U.S.A.

A Military and Naval aircraft review was held at Hendon in September, and tests continued with arming aeroplanes with machine guns and bombs. In Britain, flights were made from moving warships of the Royal Navy, from H.M.S. *Hibernia* and H.M.S. *London*. This lead in time to the modern aircraft carrier.

The monoplane now really began to go into eclipse, from which it was not to emerge as the principal type of aeroplane for many years. At this point in aircraft history, with its lift, strength, and compactness, the biplane was seen to have advantages over the monoplane, which needed larger wing surfaces. Moreover, the French and British army authorities banned the monoplane for army use, following two crashes in England and a report by Blèriot, so long the champion of the monoplane, dealing with its structural weakness. These two factors greatly retarded monoplane development, though it is said that Winston

Churchill, then First Lord of the Admiralty, refused to let the ban apply to naval aircraft. At this time the Royal Flying Corps, later to become the Royal Air Force, had not been formed. Each Service had its own aircraft 'wing' or flying force of aeroplanes.

On 30 May 1912, Wilbur Wright died, aged 45, from typhoid fever, thus removing one of the greatest figures of early aviation from the scene.

This year saw the appearance from Farnborough of the B.S.1 Scout. This was to be the basis of a type of fighter machine for many years to come. Designed chiefly by de Havilland, it was a fast, single seater biplane, with forward engine and airscrew, a cylindrical, tapered fuselage, ending in a flat tail and small, vertical rudder. It was mounted on wheels which themselves were fixed to skids.

The next year, 1913, saw the first parachute jump made from an aeroplane in Europe. Long distance flights continued to increase, both in distance and number. The Farnborough government aircraft factory produced what was classified as the first inherently stable aeroplane; one that

44. The Farnborough B.E.2, 1913, the first practical inherently stable aeroplane. The pilot sat in the rear cockpit

was reliable, practical, and much safer and easier to handle. It was to be the backbone of the force of early reconnaissance machines with which Britain entered the coming war. In all, some 2,000 were built. This fine little biplane was the Farnborough B.E.2, with a forward engine and four bladed tractor propeller. It seated two, in line, in the fuselage, and was mounted on wheels and skids.

At the same time a remarkable example of early streamlining as applied to an aeroplane appeared in the form of the Deperdussin racing monoplane. Here was a sleek machine, with all the corners removed, with a sharply tapered fuselage, low wings and an open cockpit, seating the pilot deep down, so that only his head was seen. It was a fine early example of the monocoque construction mentioned above. The engine was almost totally enclosed in the strong fuselage.

Harry Hawker, whose name is now linked with one of our greatest modern aircraft firms, designed, with F. Sigrist, the Sopwith Tabloid. A two-seater biplane, this fine little machine had an 80-h.p. Gnome engine, a top speed of 92 m.p.h., and

45. The Avro 504 two-seater biplane of 1913–14, to become, with slight modifications, one of the most famous aeroplanes in history. Note the staggered wings, derived from the Goupy II type, illustration p. 48

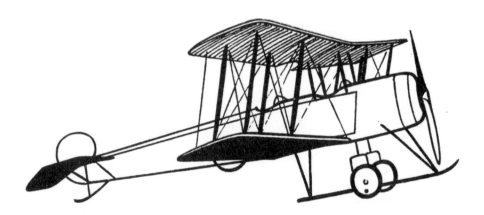

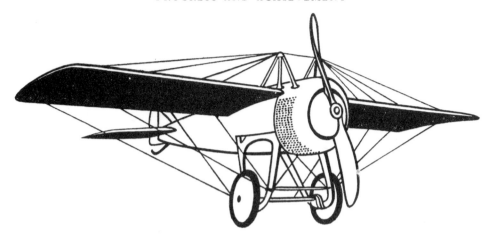

46. The Deperdussin racing monoplane of 1913

could climb to 15,000 ft. in ten minutes. It was an almost fatal blow to the monoplane school of design, at least for some years. At this period few monoplanes could match its performance. At first the Tabloid used wing warping control, but later models were fitted with ailerons.

A. V. Roe built his first Avro type 504 biplane, and in Russia, Igor Sikorsky, later to leave that country and develop the helicopter, built a large, four-engined cabin biplane which could carry up to 15 people.

In August 1913, that indefatigable pioneer,

S. F. Cody, now a British subject, was killed, with his passenger, testing a new biplane.

All this time speeds, distances, and heights reached had continued to increase. At the end of 1913, where our story must close, these stood as follows:

Speed: 126·67 m.p.h., by M. Prevost of France at Reims.

Distance: 634·54 miles non-stop, over a closed circuit, by A. Seguin of France, at Buc.

Height: 20,079 ft., by G. Legagneux of France at St. Raphael.

Thus the scene before the fatal year of 1914 when war, till then often a local affair, was to engulf much of the world, to earn the doubtful distinction of being World War I. This calamity spurred on, as war always does, technical achievements in many fields, not the least in flying. Once war has started and risk and expense are no longer of any object in the fight for survival, scientific progress becomes rapid. It is a bad reflection on civilisation that great progress should go hand-in-hand with destruction. What war did to develop flying we may, perhaps, tell in a later volume.

Index

(Items numbered in italic are illustrated)

Printed in Great Britain by Fletcher & Son Ltd, Norwich.